SENTIMENTAL JOURNEY

SONGS OF THE WORLD WAR II ERA

The Life, Times, & Music™ Series

SENTIMENTAL JOURNEY

SONGS OF THE WORLD WAR II ERA

The Life, Times, & Music™ Series

Delilah Jones

FRIEDMAN/FAIRFAX
PUBLISHERS

A FRIEDMAN GROUP BOOK

© 1994 by Michael Friedman Publishing Group, Inc.

ISBN 1-56799-134-3

THE LIFE, TIMES, & MUSIC ™ *SERIES*
SENTIMENTAL JOURNEY: *Songs from the World War II Era*
was prepared and produced by
Michael Friedman Publishing Group, Inc.
15 West 26th Street
New York, New York 10010

Editor: Sharyn Rosart
Art Director: Jeff Batzli
Designer: Kevin Ullrich
Photography Editor: Colleen Branigan

Grateful acknowledgment is given to authors, publishers, and
photographers for permission to reprint material. Every effort has been
made to determine copyright owners of photographs and illustrations. In
the case of any omissions, the publishers will be pleased to make suitable
acknowledgments in future editions.

Printed in the United States of America

Cover Photography Credits: Connie Boswell: Photofest; Trumpet: © Leo
de Wys/Sipa/Le Pautre; The Andrews Sisters: Photofest; Airplane:
© Superstock; Frank Sinatra: © NBC/Globe Photos.

For bulk purchases and special sales, please contact:
Friedman/Fairfax Publishers
Attention: Sales Department
15 West 26th Street
New York, New York 10010
(212) 685-6610 FAX (212) 685-1307

TABLE OF CONTENTS

Introduction   8

The American Home Front   10

Radio and Recording Bans   14

The Origins and Rise of Swing   22

Other Notable Bandleaders of the War Years   39

The Vocalists   42

The Vocal Groups   61

The End of the Journey   65

Suggested Listening   68

Further Reading   70

Index   71

Introduction

From 1941 to 1945 America found itself riding along on a cultural and social sentimental journey that was to change the sound and the character of popular music. Among the factors that contributed to that transformation were America's involvement in the war and the people's personal response to war itself.

Unlike the music of the First World War, which embraced songs with war themes, such as "Over There," the songs of the early 1940s did not sentimentalize war. The arrival of a *second* world war made it difficult for people to generate the same idealistic innocence the first war had inspired. The reality of so many young lives lost in the first war made it impossible to greet a second world catastrophe with equal vigor. Patriotic support for the war was expressed in public, but in their hearts people yearned for

Martha Raye entertaining American troops stationed in North Africa, 1943.
During the war years, entertainers traveled far and wide, from training camps
to the battlefield, to help boost morale.

peace. Thus, the songs of the 1940s war years sentimentalized the personal, celebrating an ideal future when loved ones separated by war would be together again or an ideal past of familiar places, friends, and family that would always be there for comfort. The start of the war marked the height of the big band era, when music could be sweet, silly, jazz-inflected, or richly orchestral. But by war's end a transformation had taken place, and Americans who once prized the bandleader and the instrument found themselves enthralled by the lilt and timbre of the human voice. The American pop vocalist was born out of the clatter and rattle of the disintegrating size and scope of the big band sound.

The American Home Front

In the early 1940s, at the height of the swing era, North Americans waited with increasing tension as Hitler's forces marched and battled their way through Europe. To escape reality, people dialed up their nearly brand-new radios to one of the CBS, NBC, or Mutual Broadcasting stations, or ventured out to dance the night away at a local dance hall or ballroom, where the delicious sounds of a jukebox or a live orchestra could be heard for relatively little money.

The political climate remained tense, however, as the theater of war widened. In September 1940, Japan invaded French Indochina. On the radio, Americans listened nightly to the swing sounds of the big bands on such programs as *Let's Dance, Make-Believe Ballroom, Your Hit Parade* (formerly *The Lucky Strike Hit Parade*), and *Kay Kyser's Kollege of Musical Knowledge*. Meanwhile, despite negotiations between the United States and Japan, tensions escalated between the two nations, and on December 7, 1941, the Japanese bombed Pearl Harbor. On December 8, Franklin Delano Roosevelt announced that Congress had declared war on Japan, and a few days later, reciprocating a declaration of war from Germany and Italy, America entered into the global struggle it had been avoiding since the late 1930s. The war machine was fired up as fifteen million men and women donned uniforms and several million more went to work in war plants. War, as it turned out, was a good antidote to the Depression. But it also changed the way the nation lived and, in turn, the nature of the music Americans heard.

War brought to the American home front gas rationing; a 35-mile-per-hour (56 kph) speed limit, to further conserve gas; and travel and entertainment restrictions in the form of a 20 percent amusement tax, which impeded the movements of audiences and touring orchestras alike.

Bands led by such greats as Glenn Miller, Benny Goodman, Tommy and Jimmy Dorsey, and Harry James could no longer afford to travel from one city to the next for back-to-back one-night stands at places like the Palomar, the Hotel Sherman, the Glen Island Casino (where it is said that swing was born when Glenn Miller and his band made an infamous appearance there

Top: Kay Kyser, a bandleader who couldn't read or write a note of music, wore a cap and gown when hosting his popular radio show, Kay Kyser's Kollege of Musical Knowledge. *Bottom: Pearl Harbor was bombed by the Japanese in December 1941—and the face of American popular music was irrevocably transformed by World War II.*

Left: Guy Lombardo, the quintessential "sweet" bandleader. Bottom: Betty Hutton performed with the Glenn Miller Band in the 1942 Twentieth Century Fox film Orchestra Wives.

and became an overnight success in 1939), the Palladium, the Aragon, and many other clubs and dance halls from New York to Los Angeles.

In the 1930s, the rise of the big band sound had been fueled by these appearances, which were often broadcast live over radio, which in turn helped boost record sales to jukebox owners. The demands of fighting a war abroad, however, stopped the touring side of the industry virtually dead in its tracks. Many of the nation's top bandleaders (and sometimes entire orchestras) joined the war effort. In April 1942, Artie Shaw enlisted in the navy, following Dean Hudson (who was the first bandleader to join up). Others soon followed: Orrin Tucker, Eddy Duchin, Claude Thornhill, Bob Crosby, Ted Weems, Alvino Rey, Sam Donahue, and Glenn Miller all joined or were drafted in 1942. Indeed, by the time war was declared in December 1941, more than two hundred bands had al-

ready signed up to entertain troops at USO functions and fund-raising rallies.

Many of these musicians served their country in Armed Services Bands. Glenn Miller, who joined the Army Air Force, formed a now legendary band to entertain the troops overseas. Some believe that it was this Army Air Force Band, far larger and more eclectic than Miller's wildly successful 1939–1942 swing band, that was his true pride and joy. Tragically, Miller died in 1944 when his plane disappeared over the Atlantic while carrying him to France, where he was headed to set up a band performance for American troops stationed there.

But the war and its direct effects (such as rationing and recruitment) did not single-handedly change the sound of American popular music in the 1940s. A number of other factors came into play from 1941 to 1943 that also contributed to the supremacy of the voice over the instrument in popular music.

Radio and Recording Bans

Radio and the recording industry both experienced growing pains in the 1930s, and at the beginning of the war, the music industry was still feeling the effects. In the 1920s, the rise of radio broadcasts of sound recordings at first adversely affected the sale of records. This was largely because until 1928, when the Federal Radio Commission required radio broadcasters to state the title of the records they played, stations routinely played music without identification. In 1929, the Artist's Protection Society required broadcasters to pay royalties for the music they aired, primarily because musicians said they were losing money from the decline in record sales. Sales of records grew strong again by the late 1930s—aided by both radio (which in the 1940s had its greatest popularity, prior to the rise of television in the 1950s) and the jukebox, which became common nationwide with improved technology. These helped make the purchase of recordings more desirable despite the effects of the Depression. But the issue of royalties did not go away.

In 1941, the radio networks got into a conflict over money with the American Society of Composers, Authors and Publishers (ASCAP). ASCAP, a group that was formed to collect royalties for its members, included such top songwriters of the day as the Gershwins, Richard Rodgers and Lorenz Hart, Cole Porter, Johnny Mercer, Harold Arlen, Jerome Kern, and Irving Berlin. By 1940, the radio- and record-listening

Kitty Kallen performing with Jimmy Dorsey and his orchestra in Four Jills in a
Jeep, *Hollywood, 1943. During the war years, many of the top orchestras traveled west in search of fame and fortune on the big screen.*

public was large enough that ASCAP felt the networks should pay more
for the license to broadcast music by its composers. Naturally, the networks refused to pay more for the same product. The result was an
ASCAP-recordings ban by the radio networks that began January 1, 1941,
and continued until October of that year. The networks, however, antici-
pating the ban before it took effect, formed their own society, Broadcast
Music International (BMI, which remains a rival to ASCAP to this day),
to represent new writers (and ASCAP defectors) and collect royalties and
license fees at terms more attractive to the broadcasters.

The initial result of the ban, however, was that bandleaders—by now
regulars or hosts of the nightly network radio programs—were forced to
scramble for material. One solution they found was to create new
arrangements for very old standards for which the rights were in the public domain (thus requiring no royalty payments). Throughout 1941, until
a settlement was eventually negotiated, the listening public was treated to
a vast array of big band and swing music devoted to such nineteenth-century titles as "I Dream of Jeanie with the Light Brown Hair," "London

Goin' Hollywood (How Hollywood and the Big Bands Got Together for a Brief, War-Effort-Induced Love Affair and Learned to Like It)

Yet another nail in the big band coffin was the call of the silver screen, which beckoned the bands in late 1942, at the height of the recording ban and amid the economically disastrous effects of the government's war-related entertainment restrictions at home.

With the exception of Benny Goodman's 1930s appearance in a film called *Hollywood Hotel* and Artie Shaw's stint a few years later in something called *Dancing Co-Ed*, the sound of swing did not make much of an appearance in Hollywood until the war years. Once Hollywood noticed it, the demand for swing was insatiable, but it was short-lived and the use of the stars of the big band scene (and

their sound) was generally inaccurate. For example, Tommy Dorsey and his orchestra appeared in a film called *Las Vegas Night* with seven brass instruments, five saxophones, and a rhythm section—only to be backed on the soundtrack by a full string section. Other films in which the musicians were used in unnatural situations include Gene Krupa's band in *Ball of Fire* and Woody Herman's in *Winter Wonderland*. Other films that featured the big bands included *The Gang's All Here*, *Swing Fever*, *Jam Session*, *Sweet and Low-Down*, *Orchestra Wives*, and *Stage Door Canteen*. Many of the films were also poorly made, which may account for their varying degrees of success at the box office.

Above: Peggy Lee and the Benny Goodman Band appeared in the 1942 film Stage Door Canteen. *Bottom: The debonair Harry James appeared in, among other films,* Best Foot Forward. *He is pictured here in a publicity still from the film with a very young Nancy Walker.*

A number of bandleaders, including Harry James, Artie Shaw, Charlie Barnet, Bob Crosby, Gene Krupa, Stan Kenton, Kay Kyser, Benny Goodman, Horace Heidt, Woody Herman, and the Dorsey brothers, all moved west at some point during the war years in search of financial and career opportunities. Though many of the films in which they appeared were of less than top quality and did nothing to further their careers, such movies as *Best Foot Forward* and *The Fleet's In* did turn out to be "gangbusters" at the box office.

Biographical films about the big band era, of which Hollywood made several during the early 1940s, focused on the lives of Glenn Miller, Gene Krupa, Benny Goodman, Eddy Duchin, and the Dorsey brothers, to name just a few. But by 1944, Hollywood's love affair with the big bands was at an end, no doubt because the films had been poorly made and the bands underused. In any event, the movies, like the American public, were about to fall in love with the classic pop sound of singers, including Doris Day, Frank Sinatra, and Bing Crosby (well—America was already enamored of Bing), all of whom would soon eclipse the bands that spawned them. Surely, though, there would have been no classic American pop vocalist sound without the overwhelming success of swing.

Bridge Is Falling Down," "My Old Kentucky Home," and "My Bonnie Lies over the Ocean," to name just a few.

Add to that the use of less-known and less-accomplished composers, the bands' inability to broadcast performances of their well-known arrangements and theme songs, and the fact that the networks effectively muzzled them with a "no ad-libbing" rule—requiring that bandleaders get approval in advance of all musical content, for fear that the musicians might get carried away and play ASCAP music by accident—and it's no wonder that listeners began to yearn for fresher sounds or, at the very least, familiar classics. As a result of the ban, bluegrass and country music experienced a small surge in popularity since this type of music was traditionally non-ASCAP material, the networks found that it was plentifully available, and audiences were ripe for new sounds.

But it was the big bands that found the situation most disadvantageous, particularly when it meant no access to the standards and theme songs with which they had made and maintained their reputations. Imagine Glenn Miller without his "Moonlight Serenade," Harry James without "Ciribiribin," Tommy Dorsey without "I'm Getting Sentimental over You," or Les Brown without his "Sentimental Journey," and it is easy to understand how hard this ban hit the bands.

Yet the ASCAP ban alone did not seal the fate of the big band sound. Directly on its heels came a far more restricting recording ban by the American Federation of Musicians (A.F. of M.) in 1942. This ban, which lasted from August 1, 1942, until early 1944, was mounted by the A.F. of M. against the radio stations and jukebox owners. It was prompted by the war and by the restrictions on travel that kept musicians from earning as much from live appearances as they had in the past (though Glenn Miller was earning $100,000 a month just from recordings in 1942 when he joined up to play for Uncle Sam), but also by the increased pres-

Top: Helen Forrest singing with Harry James and his Music Makers in 1943 at the CBS Radio Network studios in New York. James and his twenty-eight-piece orchestra replaced Glenn Miller on the network when Miller's band went off to fight the war. Bottom: Tommy Dorsey, whose consummate talents as a trombonist inspired the vocal style of Frank Sinatra.

In a 1941 production still from the film Las Vegas Nights, *a very young "un-known" Frank Sinatra (far right, back row) is just another member of the Tommy Dorsey Band.*

ence of jukeboxes in drugstores, restaurants, and bars, which meant less work for live musicians. The A.F. of M.'s only recourse for increasing their revenues was to charge more for the use of recordings of their members' work, but once again the networks and the recording companies refused to pay more.

As with the earlier ban, when the distributors refused to pay, the result was a stalemate that effectively prevented musicians from making any recordings. But since singers were unaffected by the ban, there was a marked increase in the number of *a cappella* recordings made, complete with vocal backups (of a proto-doo-wop variety), as well as just about any other accompaniment that did not fall under the jurisdiction of the A. F. of M. (Organists and harmonicists, for example, were not members of the A. F. of M.) This being wartime, the public demand for a musical sound in which to escape made this a ripe time for recording companies to try anything once if it meant creating and moving product.

This gradual and unavoidable scaling down of the big band sound contributed to the popularity of vocalists (both individually and in groups) as well as an increased interest in their personalities (as opposed to the personalities of the bandleaders). That the time was ripe for vocalists to stand out and connect directly with their audiences appears to have been serendipitous, though it might have been inevitable, considering that some of the new vocalists were one-of-a-kind stylists like Doris Day, Peggy Lee, and Frank Sinatra.

By the time the strike was settled in 1944, the recording companies had discovered a new set of stars: the vocalists. The instrumentalists were relegated to the unfamiliar role of accompanists.

In the 1940s, the very young and very handsome Frank Sinatra made young girls swoon.

The Origins and Rise of Swing

The secret to the success of the big bands in their heyday, roughly 1935 to 1944, is really the story of how swing was born. The bands of Benny Goodman, Glenn Miller, and the Dorsey brothers, the white jazz bands that led the wave of the big bands' most commercially successful years, succeeded because of a series of interrelated events and influences that conspired to create the unique sound known as swing.

Tommy Dorsey (on trombone) and Jimmy Dorsey (on saxophone) were among a handful of pioneers who helped create the sound of swing.

Among the major influences on swing were Louis Armstrong's creation of a distinctive rhythmic jazz language and techniques that made it possible for improvisational jazz to be incorporated into more mainstream musical styles, such as the insertion of syncopated sections within the regular beat, or instrumental sections that were singled out at unpredictable times—which resulted in an exciting style that greatly increased

Glenn Miller joined the Army in 1942 and formed a military band to entertain the troops overseas that to this day is remembered for its range and quality.

the opportunities for instrumental and vocal soloists to display special talents. Some might say that swing is really a word that describes jazz for a white audience.

In addition to these stylistic developments, the rise of radio at the end of the 1930s, as well as the rise of the film and recording industries, meant that an increasing number of musicians were able to find work—which meant the creation of a large talent pool from which all the big bands were able to draw. Indeed, there was a great deal of talent shifting back and forth among the bands; some combinations clicked while others didn't. During the late 1930s, as improved technology continued to increase the size of the music industry's audience, the major bandleaders jockeyed and arranged and rearranged not only personnel but also combinations within orchestras and arrangements. With constant touring and personnel changes, even the orchestra itself could begin to feel improvisational.

The swing sound broke through to the general public in 1939, when Glenn Miller and his band, whose Paul Whiteman– and Benny Goodman–influenced musical style was developed over several years, became an overnight success while performing live over the radio in a series of late-night broadcasts from the Roseland State Ballroom in Boston, the Paradise Restaurant in New York, and the now infamous Meadowbrook Ballroom in New Jersey and Glen Island Casino in New York. The secret to their newfound success was radio, which steadily increased its audience through the 1930s, and the key ingredient was the sound of swing—a sound that Benny Goodman, the "King of Swing," helped to invent (or at any rate popularize), that Glenn Miller helped to perfect, and that hundreds of others imitated.

The brassy, reedy, rhythmic swing sound is often contrasted with the romantic, sentimental sound of "sweet" bands like those formed by Guy

Benny Goodman (1909–1986)

Benny Goodman was born in Chicago, the child of Russian-Jewish immigrants who made music lessons a mandatory part of their son's education. Goodman studied clarinet with the strict classical disciplinarian Franz Schoepp, who also taught Jimmy Noone and Buster Bailey. Goodman was influenced by Schoepp as well as by the sound of local klezmer clarinetists, Johnny Dodds (who played with the King Oliver Band), and Noone.

Early on, Goodman showed a prodigious talent that, under Schoepp's tutelage, blossomed into such virtuosity of tone and style that in later years Goodman easily moved in and out of the realm of classical music. He was equally gifted as a bandleader. Indeed, it is likely that this latter talent is the real secret to Goodman's sudden and phenomenal success in 1935, when at the age of twenty-six he led his band across the country on a tour that landed him an opening-night success at Hollywood's Palomar Ballroom that most historians mark as the start of the big band era.

Benny Goodman put the sound of swing on the map in 1935 when his band's twenty-six-week appearance on the Let's Dance *radio show on NBC found a nation-wide audience.*

Goodman, who was known as the "King of Swing" for his role in launching and popularizing the sound, became a member of the Chicago musician's union when he was thirteen years old, and by his late teens he was sitting in with a number of different bands. In 1924, he began playing with Ben Pollack, with whom he made his first recordings, and in subsequent years he played with a number of distinguished bands, including Paul Whiteman's and Ted Lewis', and George Gershwin's Broadway Theatre orchestra. By the 1930s, Goodman was an experienced studio musician and freelance radio performer with a tremendous skill and consistency in handling a profusion of new songs from Tin Pan Alley, an unusual technical facility and relatively good feel for jazz, and an extraordinary series of playing opportunities that enabled him to consolidate his natural instrumental versatility.

He formed his first band in 1934 and played his first engagement with them at New York's Billy Rose Music Hall, followed by a grueling cross-country tour that nearly broke up the band along the way. But Goodman stuck to it and was rewarded with a resounding success, thanks to the increasing power of radio, when the band arrived in California in the summer of 1935. The twenty-six-week tour, broadcast live on the *Let's Dance* radio show on NBC, gradually found its audience.

Perhaps it is no coincidence that Goodman, using hip, jazzy arrangements by Fletcher Henderson, found his audience in the Pacific time zone—for *Let's Dance* aired late at night in the East, but earned a prime-time slot in the West. When the band arrived at the Palomar, following weeks of failures and disappointment, the standing-room-only crowd that greeted them was overwhelming.

For the next five years, Goodman dominated the dance music scene, turning out hundreds of hit recordings, appearing in motion pictures, and hosting such popular radio shows as *Let's Dance* and the *Camel Caravan*, the latter of which was sponsored by the National Biscuit Company.

In 1938, the band played Carnegie Hall to stomps and cheers, bringing the sound of swing into the hallowed halls of traditional classical music and, figuratively, blowing the roof off the place. In 1940, Goodman returned to Carnegie Hall for a solo performance with the New York Philharmonic, playing Mozart's Clarinet Concerto and Debussy's First Rhapsody. Goodman continued to play and record a wide variety of classical music, especially as the swing sound's popularity began to wane.

Benny Goodman's musical talent ranged from innovations as a swing artist to a 1940s appearance at Carnegie Hall with the New York Philharmonic.

In 1940, Goodman disbanded the group in order to rest and receive treatment for a troublesome back ailment. He reorganized the band several months later and once again became the leader of one of the top bands in the business, but the special feeling that had sparked the original band of the 1930s never quite returned. That feeling produced the band's hallmark, which was a synthesis of sound that emphasized the brilliance of the group over that of soloists.

Such an achievement seems even more remarkable considering that Benny Goodman, a perfectionist who was notorious for constantly altering the makeup of his band over the years, worked with some of the best individual artists in the business. Among the sidemen and singers who performed with him, many highly respected in their own right as musicians (and some as bandleaders in later years), were Gene Krupa, Harry James, Fletcher Henderson, Bunny Berigan, Red Norvo, Helen Forrest, Peggy Lee, Martha Tilton, and Patti Page.

During the 1940s, with many of the best musicians drafted into the armed forces, Goodman found it increasingly difficult to maintain a solid sound. Audience interest began to dwindle, and the band broke up for good in 1943. In the ten years they flourished, the Goodman band had managed to make over four hundred recordings, including the "King Porter Stomp" (their first hit), "Blue Skies," "Life Goes to a Party," and, with Peggy Lee recording the vocals in the 1940s, "How Long Has This Been Goin' On?" and "Blues in the Night."

Above: In the 1940s, Les Brown and his orchestra recorded numerous hits with Doris Day singing vocals, including "Sentimental Journey" and "My Dreams Are Getting Better All The Time."

Left: Jimmy Dorsey became the leader of his own swing band following an onstage falling-out with his equally talented brother, Tommy.

Lombardo (though every swing band had its "sweet" repertoire). It was a sound that never lost sight of three elements that were essential to its popularity: a smooth rhythm and arrangement, an uncomplicated composition, and sufficient contrast to keep the listener's interest. In other words, swing had a smoothed-out jazz sound that was consistent, yet colorful enough to remain both accessible and entertaining. In its heyday, swing made limited use of the human voice—after all, the ideal swing vocal was meant to blend in with the orchestra, to complement rather than stand out. Often a vocal line might even be performed by a string section, though the ideal swing band stayed within the half-dozen sonorities of the brass and reed instruments, accompanied only by a good rhythm section.

For many jazz enthusiasts, the swing sound is a pale reflection of the original, but for millions of Americans struggling through the end of the Depression, it was the only music to be heard.

During the war years, white swing bands led by such greats as Jimmy and Tommy Dorsey, Glenn Miller, Benny Goodman, Artie Shaw, Harry James, Les Brown, and Woody Herman, as well as those led by Horace Heidt, Frankie Carle, Bob Crosby, and Kay Kyser, flourished despite the

Glenn Miller (1904–1944)

Glenn Miller (foreground) and his band, featuring a uniquely fine-tooled swing sound, was hugely popular from 1939 to 1944, when Miller's army transport plane went down at sea en route to Paris.

The Glenn Miller Band's phenomenal popular success was unprecedented, both in audience attendance and record sales. Given that his band was far more popular than Benny Goodman's band before it or Kay Kyser's extremely successful radio orchestra (although Kyser himself was not a musician), Miller's untimely death in 1944 seems all the more tragic for what might have been had he survived the war, although his sudden death at the height of the war no doubt contributed to the continued popularity of his music. Despite the brevity of his tenure, Miller's contribution to swing was indelible.

His overnight success in 1939, due to a series of hugely popular live broadcasts from the Meadowbrook Ballroom and the Glen Island Casino, was as extraordinary and unexpected as Goodman's Palomar Ballroom success four years earlier. Miller's career actually began in the 1920s. Like Goodman, he played with a variety of bands, including those led by Boyd Senter and Max Fischer. Starting in 1925, he played with Ben Pollack, for whom he wrote a number of arrangements. Over the next ten years, Miller embarked upon a quest to develop a new clarinet-lead sound that did not hit pay dirt until those infamous 1939 broadcasts. A perfectionist who knew what he wanted and was willing to work until he got it, Miller honed his craft as an arranger, and in 1935, he worked as a contractor for a band led by Ray Noble at New York's Rainbow Room.

In January 1937, Miller formed his first band, and despite a positive reception at the Roosevelt in New Orleans, it disbanded by year's end. In 1938 Miller tried again, this time with a recording contract with Victor's Bluebird label. At first, sales of the recordings did poorly, but heavy coast-to-coast late-night radio broadcasts from the Roseland State Ballroom, the Paradise Restaurant, and the Meadowbrook Ballroom during the first months of 1939 delivered Miller's message to the right audience at the right time, and the unique swing sound of the Glenn Miller Band finally took off. Suddenly, the band's recordings of "In the Mood," "Moonlight Serenade" (which was to become Miller's theme song), and "Little Brown Jug" became huge hits. After ten years of trial and error, Miller's modified Goodman repertory of Henderson-style arrangements had finally gelled. The result was a unique swing sound that went down easy but always managed to be quietly surprising, a sound that featured a tightly muted brass section and a full, rich, reed-driven melody.

In the fall of 1939, the band signed a contract with Chesterfield to perform a radio show three nights a week. With these regular braodcasts, they rapidly became the most successful dance band in the world. The Miller sound was a romantic, pop sound that appealed to a wide audience and was perfectly poised to deliver just the right amount of sentimentality to a country about to go to war. It is impossible to convey the magical effect the Miller sound had on its audience; the sound Miller had worked so hard to create through the 1930s became for a brief time in the 1940s the sweetest expression of daily life, the sound that Americans most dearly wanted to hear.

In 1942, Miller enlisted in the United States Army Air Force, an act resulting from his belief that band appearances at army camps were not enough for him to do to help his country. Enlisting as a captain, Miller formed a new military band to entertain the troops, which promptly became the most popular service band in the country. Indeed, in typical Miller fashion, he resisted Army regulations and formed a forty-two-piece Army Air Force Band that included, among other assets, a nineteen-piece jazz ensemble similar to his civilian dance band. The achievement of the band was its ability to play everything from swing to jazz to works from the classical repertory without sacrificing quality. During his tenure as leader of the Army Air Force Band, until his death in 1944, Miller continued to experiment with music and even wrote new swing arrangements of traditional army marches.

Between 1939 and 1942, Miller's civilian band enjoyed a string of hits, including "Pennsylvania 6-5000," "Tuxedo Junction," "Juke Box Saturday Night," "I Got a Gal in Kalamazoo," and "Chattanooga Choo Choo," which sold a million records within six months of being issued and eventually became one of the few titles to sell in the multimillions before the advent of rock and roll. The smooth, blended, nonvibrato sound of the Modernaires, who recorded extensively with Miller's band, are yet another example of the way that he could turn a musical concept, performed with craft and taste, into a major commercial asset. It is tempting to think that, had he survived the war, Miller's canny ability to tap the commercial requirements of the popular music business might have continued to serve him during the postwar years.

challenges presented by the economic and social conditions of the day. Indeed, there were as many as four hundred fifty successful name bands during those peak years, plus several hundred less-known bands, making live radio broadcasts and touring the country to play ballrooms and hotels nationwide. Popular success was the name of the game (no surprise, given the rigors of the Depression years), and it didn't matter whether the players were a sweet, dance, hotel, society, Mickey Mouse, or novelty band—what mattered was selling records and tickets. A lack of sales would mean the demise of the bands. While the best bands could cater to a wide range of audience tastes and still retain the integrity of their own unique sound, no band could retain a wide audience when public taste had shifted to embrace a new sound. By the end of 1946, most of the major bandleaders, including Woody Herman, Benny Goodman, and Tommy Dorsey, disbanded their orchestras, unable to compete with the changing times and the changing tastes of the American public.

Above: Harry James and his Music Makers, performing in 1944 with vocalist Helen Forrest. Together, James and Forrest recorded a string of wartime hits, including "I Don't Want to Walk Without You." Right: Harry James and his Music Makers appeared in the Twentieth Century Fox film Springtime in the Rockies. *The film starred Betty Grable, who later became Mrs. Harry James.*

Kay Kyser (1906–1985)

Kay Kyser was one of the few bandleaders who was not known for his musicianship to attain great popularity in the 1940s. He was above all a showman, and his hugely popular radio show, *Kay Kyser's Kollege of Musical Knowledge*, was a pioneer in the field of game shows. Originally broadcast out of Chicago's Blackhawk Restaurant in 1934 via a local radio station, Kyser's show made a game of guessing the titles of songs, and in one brief moment, a kind of silly college pastime became a lifetime's career.

Kyser, a college buddy of the great Tin Pan Alley songwriter Johnny Mercer, began forming and leading bands as early as the late 1920s, but it was this inspired use of radio (along with aggressive marketing of the local program to the network station, Chicago's WGN, which eventually picked the program up and distributed it nationwide) that was his claim to fame. As the show gained a wider audience, Kyser expanded it, adding various novelty and comedy routines, including the invention of zany characters such as "Ishkabibble" (who was played by an excellent trumpeter whose real name was Merwyn Bogue) and music that made lamentable use of sugary saxes and clip-clopping brass. Good music was hardly the point as far as Kyser was concerned—the point was entertainment. Indeed, by the early 1940s, Kyser's band was probably the biggest attraction in the business, in demand everywhere for concert appearances, dance dates, and theater engagements, setting attendance records everywhere it appeared.

During the war years, Kyser did his stint performing for the troops and participating in USO shows at army bases and war plants, originating each of his weekly radio programs from some such installation. Some of the novelty numbers that Kyser's band was known for include "Three Little Fishes," "Who Wouldn't Love You?" and "Praise the Lord and Pass the Ammunition" (the band's most famous recording and a number one record in 1943). In the early 1940s, Kyser worked with two of his best-known vocalists: Harry Babbitt, who never sang distinctively but always sang well, and Ginny Sims, an attractive woman with a smooth voice and intelligent delivery of lyrics.

Despite Kyser's lack of musical talent, by 1942 he put together an outstanding band that included such top jazz-style musicians as Noni Bernardi, Herbi Haymer, and Roc Hillman. In addition to its novelty recordings, the Kyser band recorded a number of sweet songs, including "Can't Get Out of This Mood" in 1942.

Top: Kay Kyser's Kollege of Musical Knowledge *always united the silly with the sublime. Bottom: Kyser's popularity eventually led to starring roles in the movies, including this appearance in MGM's* Right About Face, *which also featured Kyser band regulars Solly Mason (left) and Ishkabibble (right).*

The Dorsey Brothers

Tommy Dorsey (1902–1956) and Jimmy Dorsey (1904–1957) grew up in the coal country around Shenandoah, Pennsylvania. Their strict bandmaster father trained them both to be cornetists, but Tommy became one of the most memorable trombonists of the swing era and Jimmy a widely respected alto saxophonist and clarinetist. When they were teenagers they formed their first band together, Dorsey's Novelty Six (later known as Dorsey's Wild Canaries), one of the first jazz bands to broadcast over radio.

The brothers made their recording debut with a band called the Scranton Sirens, though they made a more lasting impression in 1924 on recordings with a very hot white dance band of the 1920s called the California Ramblers. They worked with a number of sturdy bandleaders, including Ben Pollack, Red Nichols, and Jean Goldkette. Soon they drew the attention of Paul Whiteman, leader of the largest, most popular, highest-paid band of the period. During this same period, the brothers established themselves as sturdy freelance studio musicians, and as radio began to grow in the 1930s, they found plenty of work with orchestra leaders on radio and in the studio.

The brothers formed a band in 1934, their first full-time professional band since their teenage effort. Unfortunately, in a famous public disagreement on the stage of the Glen Island Casino in 1935, it became clear that a professional union of the brothers was not meant to be. After disagreeing about which arrangement should come next in the middle of that famous concert, Tommy walked off the stage and never looked back. In 1935, the Dorsey Brothers Orchestra became the Jimmy Dorsey Orchestra; Tommy hired twelve former members of the Joe Haymes Orchestra and launched the Tommy Dorsey Orchestra that same year.

Both brothers' bands found their greatest success in the early 1940s. Jimmy's orchestra hit it big in 1941 with recordings of "Amapola" (which sold ninety thousand copies in one week), "Yours," "Green Eyes" (which was an overnight sensation and sold in the multimillions), and "Tangerine." Featuring the boy- and girl-next-door sound of vocalists Bob Eberly and Helen O'Connell, Jimmy's band flowed neatly with the mood of the nation as it shifted from the instrumental pyrotechnics of the 1930s to the subdued, romantic ballads Jimmy chose for his attractive singers. When O'Connell left the band in 1943 to concentrate on raising her family, Jimmy replaced her with Kitty Kallen, and the formula held—audiences were equally pleased by the sentimental duets Jimmy selected Kitty to sing with Eberly.

Tommy's orchestra fared even better, becoming one of the best all-around dance bands in the country. Known as "The Sentimental Gentleman of Swing," Tommy became a master of creating moods—and sentimental moods were exactly what appealed to a restless nation at war. Tommy also managed to work with some of the best singing talent of his day, including Frank Sinatra (whom he stole from Harry James, with Harry's blessing), Jo Stafford, and the Pied Pipers. Among the Tommy Dorsey Orchestra's greatest recordings were "For Sentimental Reasons," "Marie," "Once in a While," "This Love of Mine," "Street of Dreams," and "There Are Such Things."

Throughout 1940, the year Sinatra joined the band, Tommy's orchestra got better and better. In fact, during the 1940s, Tommy was in demand wherever big bands appeared. During the war years, Tommy augmented the size of his band substantially, bringing in an all-female string section of twenty, with the string section being larger than the size of his entire band in the 1930s. (This bit of

Top: Tommy Dorsey (on trombone) and his orchestra. Bottom: Jimmy Dorsey. The Dorsey Brothers split up in 1935 while performing live at the Glen Island Casino, and did not play together again until 1953.

schmaltz may have been an attempt to wring as much sentiment as possible out of the moment, for as soon as the war ended the string section disappeared.)

The intense rivalry between the Dorsey brothers extended beyond the bandstand, and occasionally erupted into violence. Nevertheless, in the spring of 1953, they reconciled and even formed a band together again (even though bands, by this time, were much less popular, they managed somehow to succeed). The new band was called The Tommy Dorsey Orchestra Featuring Co-Leader Jimmy Dorsey. Jackie Gleason got them a weekly television show in 1954, on which they introduced stars of the new generation such as Elvis Presley. For the next two years, their show was possibly the biggest television program built around a dance band, and this popularity encouraged other bandleaders to seek opportunities on television.

The happy reunion ended in November 1956, when Tommy died in his sleep. Jimmy, who had been suffering from cancer, apparently lost his will to live and died within a year, in June 1957. Ironically, Jimmy's final recording, "So Rare," made earlier that year, leapt to the top of the Hit Parade and stayed there. Its popularity was a testament to the musical power of the Dorsey brothers.

Harry James (1916–)

Harry James was Benny Goodman's trumpeter from late in the summer of 1936 until early 1939, when he left Goodman's band to form his own orchestra. At first, James' orchestra played smaller spots for less pay while it worked itself into shape. In the summer of 1939, James discovered and signed up a new singer, Frank Sinatra, although six months later he released Sinatra from his contract to go and sing with the more successful Tommy Dorsey Orchestra. James, unfazed, replaced Sinatra with a young singer named Dick Haymes, who proved just fine for the new orchestra's needs.

Indeed, Harry James' orchestra took a few years to find its audience. But once it did, with a string of recordings starting in May 1941 and continuing through the war years, James' orchestra became firmly established as one of the top swing bands in the business. Among the hits for which the band is known are recordings of "You Made Me Love You," "How High the Moon," "Fools Rush In," "The Nearness of You," and "I've Heard That Song Before." Once he found his rhythm, so to speak, James' formula for success consisted of schmaltzy arrangements tailored to his trumpet and the vocal needs of whoever was singing for him at the time.

Besides his successful series of recordings with Haymes, his best collaboration was with singer Helen Forrest, who joined James' orchestra following fallings-out with Artie Shaw and Benny Goodman. Forrest and James worked well together from late 1941 until the summer of 1943, when James married Betty Grable and the band's direction lost some of its focus.

Among the sentimental swing hits that James recorded with Forrest were a series of songs about boys in the service and their girls back home: "I Don't Want to Walk Without You," "My Beloved Is Rugged," "Make Love to Me," and "I Had the Craziest Dream." When Glenn Miller enlisted, James' band took his place on Chesterfield's radio show, and in the summer of 1942, the band was voted the number one group in the country on *Make-Believe Ballroom*.

After the war, James, like many of his contemporaries, called it quits in the face of so many changes in the nation's musical tastes. But he was unable to stay away too long; he eventually reorganized the band (minus the strings) and has managed to keep himself busy ever since. Not bad for an old trumpet player.

Harry James began his career as a trumpeter with the Benny Goodman Band. In 1939, he went on to create his own, highly respected orchestra, which recorded a string of hits in the early 1940s.

Helen Forrest and Harry James (right) pose for a CBS radio network publicity still. In 1942, James' orchestra was voted the number one band in the country.

Other Notable Bandleaders of the War Years

Other notable bandleaders of the war years who deserve mention include Les Brown, whose tag line was "Les Brown and the Band of Renown"; Horace Heidt, known as "Horace Heidt and His Musical Knights"; and Frankie Carle, whose theme song was "Sunrise Serenade."

Les Brown's band, formed in 1938, was one of the sturdiest, most popular bands of the war years. Together with Doris Day, Brown recorded several songs that to this day define the era, including "Sentimental Journey," "Just One of Those Things," and "I've Got My Love to Keep Me Warm," which was recorded during the war but sat in Columbia's files until 1948, when Brown revived the song in a live performance and piqued some interest; along with "Sentimental Journey," it was one of his biggest hits. Brown's band was an arranger's band that made its soloists look good, which may account for Brown's success dur-

Les Brown and his orchestra performing with regular vocalist Doris Day at the Log Cabin in New York, 1941.

ing the war years, a time when audiences were increasingly interested in soloists. During the postwar years, his band appeared on Bob Hope's radio show and later on Hope's television show. Like many of his contemporaries, Brown disbanded in 1946 only to reorganize a new, smaller version of the band the following year. Today, as interest in the sound of the big bands resurges, Brown's music is still in demand. Some other hits he recorded with Doris Day include "My Dreams Are Getting Better All the Time" and "You Won't Be Satisfied."

Horace Heidt's origins were in vaudeville. His first band included a trained dog. Although during the 1920s and early 1930s he directed one of the most entertaining bands of the period, in the 1940s Heidt specialized in the corny. His first radio show, in 1936, featured a fourteen-piece orchestra, a glee club, the singing guitar of Alvino Rey, and the King Sisters. His second show, *Pot of Gold*, was one of the first radio give-

Top: In 1941, Horace Heidt performs at the piano with two of his favorite vocalists, Mimi Cabanne (left) and Donna Wood (center). Bottom: The Horace Heidt Orchestra, circa 1934, included a trained dog and a guy in a mule costume.

away shows. The show was so popular it inspired a film, which also featured the band and all the program's stars. During the war years, Heidt hired some of the best swing musicians around, especially members of Glenn Miller's band when Miller went off to serve the country. Following a drawn-out battle with the Music Corporation of America over the handling of his business affairs, Heidt retired in late 1943 and stayed relatively free of the music business for a while. In 1946, he started yet another popular show, this time for television, called *The Youth Opportunity Show*—an amateur hour that was highly successful. Heidt, like Kay Kyser, was a consummate showman.

Frankie Carle (on piano) played with Horace Heidt's orchestra until 1944, when he left to start his own band.

Frankie Carle was a regular member of Horace Heidt's orchestra in the early 1940s and even became his co-leader in 1943. Carle's talent was of the novelty genre as well: He played the piano with his hands behind his back. But he was more than just a guy with a gimmick, and he had aspirations to form his own band. So with Heidt's blessing, Carle formed a good band, which had its debut at the Café Rouge in the Hotel Pennsylvania, New York, in February 1944. His theme song, "Sunrise Serenade," featured him at the piano. His playing was simple and straightforward, ideally suited for hotel and ballroom dancing.

The Vocalists

Bing Crosby, Frank Sinatra, Peggy Lee, Kate Smith, Dinah Shore, Jo Stafford, Doris Day, and to a certain extent, Helen Forrest, Dick Haymes, Helen O'Connell, Perry Como, and Betty Hutton—these are the vocalists of the 1930s and 1940s whose distinctive individual styles broke through the orchestral sounds of the big bands they sang with (that is, with the exception of Dinah Shore and Kate Smith, who were among the few pop singers of the 1940s who did not train on tour, on radio, or in the recording studio with a big band), who defined the sentimental sound of the

Top: Vocalist Martha Tilton mugs for the camera during a rehearsal with the Benny Goodman Orchestra for a 1938 radio broadcast over CBS. Middle: Harry Babbitt, who sang with Kay Kyser's band in the early 1940s. Bottom: Popular 1930s big band vocalist Betty Hutton emerged as a major film star in the 1940s.

Bing Crosby (1903–1977)

Bing Crosby, performing with the Paul Whiteman Orchestra as part of a featured trio called the Rhythm Boys, made his movie debut in 1930 in a film called King of Jazz.

Bing Crosby (born Harry Lillis Crosby, Jr.) began his crooning career in 1925 when he dropped out of college to try to make it as a singing duo with his partner Alton Rinker in California's vaudeville circuit. Aided by Rinker's sister, Mildred Bailey (the first featured female vocalist with a major national dance band), the duo had a pretty easy time of it. With her contacts and quite a lot of her material, the singing duo landed a gig within a year and a half with the Paul Whiteman Orchestra, the most popular dance orchestra in the country at that time. The duo did well with Whiteman until the tour arrived at Manhattan's Paramount Theater, where the manager found their singing style too jazzy for his and his audience's tastes, and the two were relegated to the back of the band. When Whiteman arranged for the boys to improve their style by working with singer-pianist Harry Barris, the duo ended up joining Barris in a trio called The Rhythm Boys. Using arrangements by Matty Malneck, the trio developed a light, swinging style that eventually became one of the most popular features of the Paul Whiteman Orchestra's stage, radio, and recording performances.

A 1930 appearance by Whiteman's orchestra in a Hollywood film called *King of Jazz* introduced Bing to the movies. (He almost lost his first film break—he was arrested for drunk driving and sentenced to thirty days in jail upon his arrival in Hollywood, then given permission to work off his debt to society by night and toil on the set by day.) When filming was completed and Whiteman's band returned to the road for a national tour, The Rhythm Boys stayed behind in Hollywood, at Bing's urging, to seek their fortune. While they remained there, Bing appeared in a number of Mac Sennett shorts and other studio films by day, and sang with the boys at the Cocoanut Grove by night. When CBS radio offered him a nightly solo network spot out of New York City in 1931, however, he abandoned the Boys to take advantage of the opportunity and became, via the air waves, a nationwide success.

In 1932, Crosby returned to Hollywood for a leading role in a movie about radio called *The Big Broadcast*. The success of that film led to a long-term contract with Paramount, which in turn led to screen stardom for Bing in a series of lighthearted musical comedies written especially to capitalize on his easygoing manner and singing style. Despite his film success, however, he continued to reach his largest audience through radio—which continued to grow throughout the 1930s—as audiences delighted in the ad-libbed quality of his appearances (he despised rehearsals) and his way of making it all seem personal. During this time his fame grew rapidly, and Paramount spared no expense in hiring top songwriting teams to write songs for him. Among the hits written expressly for the singer were "Moonlight Becomes You," "A Pocketful of Dreams," and "Swingin' on a Star." Crosby's phenomenal success in the 1930s, following years of training on the nightclub circuit with large orchestras, gave rise to such singers as Perry Como, Frank Sinatra, and Peggy Lee—all of whom got their start with the big bands before they made names for themselves as solo singers in the 1940s.

In the late 1930s, Crosby was teamed with comedian Bob Hope in a series of "road" movies that made the pair famous. For the next twenty-three years, *The Road to Singapore, Zanzibar, Morocco, Rio, Utopia, Bali,* and *Hong Kong* was always littered with their quips and camaraderie. During the war years, Bob Hope (with Bing often at his side) spearheaded hundreds of USO performances for the troops at home and abroad. Despite their popular success as a com-

edy team, it was Crosby's solo performances in such well-regarded films as *Going My Way* and *The Bells of St. Mary's* that earned him a reputation as more than a crooner with a quick ad-lib.

Today he is best remembered for the mellifluous, honey tone of his voice, and for his radio broadcasts to millions of adoring fans during the 1930s and '40s. The combination of familiarity and sentimental gentleness of Bing Crosby's voice in songs like "I'll Be Seeing You," the number one song in 1944, captures the unique sound of the era.

Bing Crosby was the quintessential radio crooner in the 1930s and 1940s.

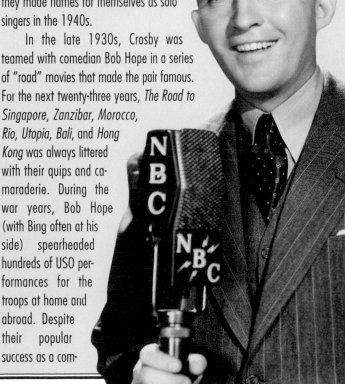

war years. Nostalgic, romantic, wistful, and familiar, the American classic pop sound emphasized phrasing and individuality of expression—it exploited the personal and the intimate rather than the large and the lush.

The touring life of the big-band singer wasn't easy, however. While on tour, band singers contended with the worst possible performance conditions including out-of-tune pianos, poor microphone and sound systems in remote locations, close living conditions on the road (often the women had to apply makeup on the bus), bands that played too loud or out of tune, and poor musical arrangements (often written for the last vocalist who rode with the band)—but the experience they gained on tour turned them into genuine craftsmen and -women. Band singers learned the importance of interplay with instrumentalists, of working closely with an arrangement, and of making the best of a less-than-ideal situation. Perhaps it is precisely the difficulty of the conditions that caused so many song stylists to blossom—a "thrive or die" situation where the only way to make the most of the experience was to rise above it.

Left: Before the fans went wild for Elvis and the Beatles, Frank Sinatra was the prototype for the male vocalist whose sex appeal could drive the crowds to distraction.
Top: Eddy Howard.
Right: Betty Hutton had appearances in a string of motion pictures, including the starring role in Annie Get Your Gun.

Frank Sinatra (1915–)

In the early years of his career, Sinatra found himself tossed in with a trio of singers from Hoboken, and he toured the country for a brief period in a quartet dubbed the Hoboken Four.

Born and raised in Hoboken, New Jersey, Frank Sinatra is a small-town kid made good. Before turning to a singing career in the mid-1930s, when he saw a Bing Crosby movie and was inspired to become a singer, Sinatra—like his father before him—worked in a variety of unskilled manual labor jobs. But in 1935, Sinatra won the *Major Bowes Original Amateur Hour*, a popular competition of the day. Sinatra won in the soloist category, while a trio of singers who also hailed from Hoboken won in the group category, so Bowes united the winners in a group and called them the Hoboken Four. He sent the quartet on an am-

ateur tour around the country, and even included them in a few movie shorts as well. But Sinatra, a born soloist, quit the tour after three months.

In 1937, he got his first regular booking at the Rustic Cabin Nightclub in Englewood, New Jersey, using the name Frankie Trent. He performed there for over a year and built a good reputation for himself in the process, eventually drawing the attention of Harry James, who signed him on with his new band. Sinatra made his first recordings with the James band, including his first version of "All or Nothing at All," but the records did poorly, and in 1940, Sinatra joined the far better Tommy Dorsey Orchestra. This was to be a turning point in his life.

Tommy Dorsey, an incomparable trombonist with amazing breath control, was to have a profound effect upon the young Sinatra. A jazz-influenced singer with a new type of free and natural phrasing, Sinatra was very impressed with Dorsey's physical control, and from the start he undertook to imitate the bandleader's trombone playing with his voice. But Sinatra was already a lot like his idol. Both had an instinctive sense of timing— "natural time" as it was called by musicians—a perfect feeling for the music. Plus, Sinatra had an earthy, rich baritone—a startling departure from the norm of the day— which favored colorless male voices that were selected for their ability to blend, to convey little expression, and to let the instruments do the talking. Everyone wanted to sing like Bing Crosby except Frank, who wanted only to be as famous as the older star. A star is exactly what Sinatra became while singing with the Tommy Dorsey Orchestra.

Undertaking to sing like Dorsey's trombone, Sinatra trained his voice to imitate the smoothness of the ballroom dance-band style and worked hard to increase his physical strength so that he, like Dorsey, could sing long phrases without pausing for breath. He increased his breath control through a rigorous training program of swimming underwater and through a Japanese breathing technique. Sinatra even trained his voice to slide languidly, like a trombone, from phrase to phrase and tone to tone.

The 1940s radio singers were the first group of singers to make casual use of the microphone (Bing Crosby and Rudy Vallee used microphones, but not with the same ease that Sinatra did), which increased their ability to convey intimacy and familiarity. Sinatra was no exception; in a booklet entitled "Tips on Popular Singing," he informed his readers that the microphone is a singer's instrument.

From 1940 to 1942, while he was singing with the Tommy Dorsey Orchestra, Frank Sinatra became a jukebox star. His fluid singing style and ease at the microphone translated as pure sexuality to his fans. He recorded 83 songs with Dorsey, including at least a dozen hits, including "I'll Never Smile Again,"

"Let's Get Away from It All," "Imagination," "Stardust," and "This Love of Mine." Not even Bing Crosby had experienced the kind of success Sinatra found among the lonely bobby-soxers who were missing their soldier boyfriends. The girls literally swooned at his live appearances, overcome by their desire to be close to him. Sinatra's huge popularity waned somewhat when the boys came home from the war—though that was largely because he failed to change his material with the times, pressing on with more and more novelty numbers although the swooning, sentimental journey of the war years had clearly come to an end.

In the 1950s Sinatra made a comeback, both in films and in musical style, rediscovering himself in assertive, upbeat songs like "I've Got the World on a String" and "Come Fly with Me." These years are commonly referred to as "the Capitol years," for the recordings he made with Capitol Records, a company that was founded by Tin Pan Alley great Johnny Mercer. With Capitol, Sinatra shed the romance of the war years for the punchy, direct style with which he is most associated today. In 1960, he founded Reprise Records to preserve and maintain complete control of his work. He remains today one of the most distinctive male vocal stylists of American popular music.

Sinatra used his microphone like an instrument, playing it for all the intimacy it could deliver to his listeners.

Doris Day (1924–)

Doris Day was a singer in the Les Brown Orchestra years before she became Rock Hudson's costar in the fabulous films of the fifties. Her singing style, like that of many of the vocalists who emerged from behind the rhythm section during the war years, was easygoing, intimate, and as close to speaking as possible without losing any of the girlish tone that was her trademark.

The only female singer of her generation to become a major star as both a recording artist and a film actress, Doris Day actually got her first break when she was eleven years old—as a dancer. She and a partner won the grand prize at a Cincinnati amateur dance contest in 1935, and she might have gone on to become a dancer were it not for a locomotive accident when she was fourteen that seriously injured her legs. While recuperating, she became determined to become a singer. Two years later, bandleader Barney Rapp hired her after hearing her sing at an amateur contest in Cincinnati. It was Rapp who turned Doris von Kappelhoff into Doris Day. But within months of her debut with Rapp, where she first sang her signature song "Day After Day," Bob Crosby (Bing's brother and a successful bandleader in his own right) stole her away from Rapp to sing with his band. Doris Day was sixteen years old and was already working on radio in New York City.

America's love affair with the motion picture sound and image of Doris Day began in 1948, when she took her first starring film role in Warner Brothers' Romance on the High Seas.

When Crosby had to let Day go soon after she arrived (a radio sponsor didn't like the sound of her voice), the singer was quickly signed up by Les Brown, with whose orchestra she recorded her biggest hits. Day sang with Brown's orchestra for six years, except for a hiatus when she was seventeen, when she quit the business and got married to Al Jorden, Rapp's trombonist. But she returned and went on to record with the Les Brown Orchestra such hits as "My Dreams Are Getting Better All the Time" and "Sentimental Journey" (a number one record of 1944 and 1945).

In 1946, Doris Day left the Les Brown Orchestra for Hollywood, where her early film roles relied heavily on her sultry but sweetly innocent singing voice, which was unnecessary, since Day turned out to be a good actress, too. Early films proved her ability to portray serious roles, though she became most famous for her 1950s and early 1960s bedroom comedies with Rock Hudson, Cary Grant, and Clark Gable. In 1968, when her third husband (Marty Melcher, who was also her business manager) died suddenly of a heart attack, she discovered that he had embezzled her entire life savings of twenty million dollars. She supported herself with a network television series and, though it took six years, successfully sued her late husband's business partner for twenty-two million dollars in damages.

Doris Day began singing with bands and on radio in the 1940s when she was still a teenager, but her image as the sweet, virginal girl-next-door was a Hollywood creation of the 1950s.

Tommy Dorsey's vocalist Connie Haines.

Dinah Shore (1917–1994)

Dinah Shore, like Kate Smith and Nat King Cole, was one of a few vocalists whose careers were not inextricably linked with the big bands of the 1930s and 1940s. Born Frances Rose Shore on March 1, 1917, in a small Tennessee town near Nashville, she adopted a dreamy, southern singing style known in the South as "noodling." After hearing Ethel Waters' recording of the song "Dinah," Shore adopted the name. Following a successful stint singing on Nashville's WSM radio station, she ventured to New York City in 1938 in search of a singing career.

Dinah Shore got her first big break singing on Eddie Cantor's network radio program in 1940, where she debuted the hit song "Yes, My Darling Daughter."

The first job Shore landed in New York, on the Lennie Hayton Orchestra's radio program, paid fifty dollars a week, but the show was canceled before it aired. She then took a nonpaying job on WNEW and worked alongside the as-yet-unknown Frank Sinatra until her big break came when one of Eddie Cantor's daughters heard her singing on WNEW and recommended Shore to her father for his network radio show. A few weeks after she debuted on Cantor's program, Shore was offered a recording contract with RCA Victor. Cantor himself paid $750 for the rights to "Yes, My Darling Daughter" for her, which became her first hit, in 1940. It was a sign of the times that Shore could succeed without a single moment's experience on the boards or on the road with one of the big bands.

By the end of 1940, just two years after her arrival in New York, Dinah was voted Outstanding New Star of the Year by six hundred radio editors polled by the New York *World-Telegram.* In 1943, she made her movie debut in the Eddie Cantor musical *Thank Your Lucky Stars*—for which her brown hair was dyed off-blonde, the color it remained thereafter. In that film she introduced another hit song, "How Sweet You Are," which was later featured on the radio program *Your Hit Parade.* In 1944, she starred opposite Danny Kaye in *Up in Arms,* in which she sang two more hits, "Now I Know" and "Tess's Torch Song." Despite these successes, her movie career never really took off. In the 1950s, television succeeded in making her a superstar where Hollywood had failed.

Throughout the war years Dinah recorded numerous hit songs, including "Blues in the Night" and "I'll Walk Alone"—songs that capitalized on her bluesy, intimate vocal style. As was typical of the era, she also recorded a number of silly, novelty songs, including "Shoofly Pie and Apple Pandowdy" and "Buttons and Bows." But whether she was serious or silly, Dinah Shore was always on top. The number one female jukebox star during the war years, her earnings from recordings and radio performances made her one of America's highest-paid female entertainers of the 1940s.

Kate Smith (1909–1986)

Say the name Kate Smith and almost anyone will reply "God Bless America." That Irving Berlin song was introduced by Smith in 1939 and is the song with which she is most closely associated after "The White Cliffs of Dover," despite the fact that Smith's name was well known to American listeners long before the Berlin song became inextricably linked with it.

She was a large woman with a voice that was naturally bright and rich. She popularized numerous songs on radio and later on television. Smith was no sex symbol but she could deliver a lyric with heartfelt expression. She had a small-town, personal style that made her listeners feel that they knew her. Her radio billing as "The Songbird of the South" contributed to that image, even though she was raised in Washington, D.C.

The superlative Kate Smith had a huge heart and a voice to match.

Smith got her start via the Broadway theater, one of a handful of 1940s pop stars who did not pay their dues with the big bands of the 1930s. Her first role was a small one in a 1926 show called *Honeymoon Lane*, in which she sang a song called "Half a Moon" and was hailed by the *New York Times* as a hit. In 1927, this big, white blues singer played a mammy in Vincent Youman's musical *Hit the Deck* and was featured in that show's most popular number, a song called "Hallelujah."

In 1930, George White cast her as the mail-order fiancée of *Flying High* star Bert Lahr. Unfortunately, constant jibes from Lahr about her weight prompted her to forsake her stage career after that show closed. In any event, she was offered a recording contract from Columbia and a CBS radio network spot four nights a week, so the time had come for Smith to move on. It was 1931 and she was all of twenty-two years old.

During the 1930s, Kate's records sold steadily and by 1933, she was earning three thousand dollars a week in radio. Though she made cameo appearances in a number of Hollywood films, her medium was radio. Smith's solid, cheerful radio manner and singing style was what Americans most wanted to hear. Among her hit songs were "Fine and Dandy," "Did You Ever See a Dream Walking," "The White Cliffs of Dover," "I'll Be Seeing You," and "It Was So Beautiful." When Kate sang "God Bless America" in 1939 on her radio program, it caused a sensation and became an instant hit.

During the war years, Smith continued making regular radio broadcasts and added live performances at shipyards, army and navy bases, war plants, and hospitals. She helped sell more than $600 million in war bonds nationwide and became, in the 1940s, an outspoken conservative political speaker.

Top: Bing Crosby (left) performing on an NBC radio program in 1948 with
Paul Whiteman (far right), Harry Parris, and Al Rinker. Whiteman gave
Crosby his first big break in the late 1920s. Bottom: Dick Haymes, the quintes-
sential young singer.

Perry Como (1913–)

Perry Como typified the bland big-band singer of the 1930s when he joined Ted Weems' highly popular dance band in 1936. From Weems he learned the importance of simple, direct communication with the audience. Indeed, Como never did quite overcome the "curse" of being one of the most pleasant singers of his era. A shy, conservative man with a full head of dark hair and an attractive face and manner, Como lacked sparkle, which ultimately cost him a career in films (despite a seven-year contract with Twentieth Century Fox in the 1940s) even if it did not prevent him from attaining moderate success as a pop singer during the war years.

In 1943, Perry Como starred on NBC's Chesterfield Supper Club, *where his pleasant vocal style won him millions of fans.*

Among his more popular recordings with Weems from 1936 to 1941 were "Picture Me Without You," "Goody Good-bye," "Until Today," and "Good Night, Sweet Dreams." But when the United States entered the war, Weems enlisted and the orchestra was disbanded. Despite having managed to keep his head above water as a singer, Como, who had trained as a barber, decided it was time to quit the business. Although he had planned to return to his hometown in Pennsylvania to open a barber shop, he instead accepted a radio contract for a late-afternoon program on CBS. There, despite his blandness, Como was turned into a major success by CBS' public relations machine. Capitalizing on the huge and sudden success that Frank Sinatra was enjoying as a romantic crooner, the radio network set Como up as a contender for the affections of all those lonely girls at home. It worked, and in 1943, Como moved to NBC to star three nights a week on its nightly *Chesterfield Supper Club* program (the other two nights the program starred Jo Stafford, lead singer of the Pied Pipers, who performed with Tommy Dorsey and his orchestra in the early 1940s alongside Frank Sinatra). Over the next four years, Como turned the program into one of the most popular music-only programs on the air.

By 1945, the pleasant crooner had sold two million records with a pair of hits, "If I Loved You" and "Till the End of Time." The key to this success was, no doubt, the songs' unabashed sentimentality. For all of his blandness, Como's ability to touch his listeners served him well. What he may have lacked in flair (as compared with Sinatra) he more than made up for with his ability to select a mix of old and new song titles whose appeal cut across the generations. Como gave his audience the security of a pleasant voice that would never shock, a smooth sound that would always comfort. Next to Bing Crosby, Como had the highest number of hit records on the charts from 1944 to 1955.

Top: Perry Como is accompanied by a harp during a 1940s recording session. Among Como's sweet hits of the period were "I'm Always Chasing Rainbows," "Prisoner of Love," and "Don't Let the Stars Get in Your Eyes." Bottom: Guy Lombardo and his orchestra perform on NBC Radio's Your Hit Parade in the 1940s, a weekly survey of the nation's favorite songs. Guest vocalist Eileen Barton joins the band, which was known for its sweet and sentimental style.

Peggy Lee (1920–)

Peggy Lee was one of the most hypnotic pop singers of the 1940s. Her signature purr of a voice draws listeners in to her intimate boudoir sound, as her lilting rhythm swings along. Often compared with Billie Holiday, Lee claims Maxine Sullivan as her biggest influence, for both Sullivan's economy of style and her simplicity of delivery.

She was born Norma Deloris Egstrom in Jamestown, North Dakota, and received the stage name Peggy Lee from the program director of a local radio station where she worked when she was in high school. Upon her graduation, she left North Dakota to pursue a singing career, and eventually wound up singing with the Will Osborne Orchestra. In 1941, while appearing at the Ambassador Hotel in Chicago, Lee got her big break when Benny Goodman saw her performance and promptly signed her up to replace Helen Forrest in his orchestra.

Among the hits she recorded with Goodman was the 1943 "Why Don't You Do Right?" which capitalized on the intense sex appeal of her creamy vocal style.

Lee's experience with Goodman's and other dance bands in the 1930s and 1940s gave her an impeccable sense of timing and rhythm. She also learned from her band experience the art of the understated phrase. Lee apparently learned something about songwriting, too, while she was paying her dues on the road, for in the mid-1940s she became the only important female pop singer of her generation to achieve note as a songwriter.

Among the songs she has written, mainly in collaboration with composers for whom she wrote lyrics, are "The Heart Is a Lonely Hunter" (Dave Grusin), the theme song for *The Russians Are Coming, The Russians Are Coming* (Johnny Mandell), and the entire score for the Disney animated feature *Lady and the Tramp* (Sonny Burke).

Peggy Lee's trademark purr went down nicely with her feline beauty, and complemented cornettist Jack Webb's jazzy horn playing and the sounds of Benny Goodman's band.

Even in the early days of her career, Peggy Lee's vocal quality was as hypnotic as her sensuality.

Helen Forrest

Helen Forrest was the quintessential "girl singer." She sang with Artie Shaw, Benny Goodman, and Harry James between 1939 and 1943, though she had her greatest success with James' orchestra. Among the hit recordings Forrest made with James (and, often, James' male vocalist Dick Haymes) were "I Had the Craziest Dream," "Skylark," "I Cried for You," "I've Heard That Song Before" (an instrumental version of which Woody Allen featured in the soundtrack of his film *Hannah and Her Sisters*), and "I Don't Want to Walk Without You." In 1942 and 1943, she was the most popular female singer in the country, according to polls conducted by *Down Beat* and *Metronome* magazines.

When Harry James eloped with Betty Grable in 1943, Forrest saw an opportunity to set out on her own as a female vocalist in pursuit of Peggy Lee's and Jo Stafford's earlier solo successes. But apart from a successful radio program with Dick Haymes from 1944 to 1947, Forrest did not manage to break out of the band singer mold. Though she blamed her failure on not being beautiful enough or, later, when rock and roll came along, hip enough, no doubt it was her ability to front a band without upstaging the music that left her unable to convert her solo status to stardom. Her warm, sweet, flexible voice adapted to any mood or expression, making her the ideal swing vocalist even if she did fall short of becoming a pop classic.

Helen Forrest's consummate skill as a band singer adept at blending in may be the reason she never attained the solo success she ardently pursued and desired in the mid-1940s.

The Vocal Groups

There were a number of innovations in vocal sound during the late 1930s and early 1940s. As musicians worked to perfect the smooth, homoge nous rhythms of swing, composers and singing groups were experimenting with the placement of melody lines and the uses of harmony. This development resulted in a sound that had its roots in the nineteenth-century barbershop quartets.

By the 1890s, after almost fifty years of development in minstrel shows, tent shows (known as traveling chautauquas), and other types of traveling vocal groups, the musical structure of the barbershop quartet was already fully formed even though the name "barbershop quartet" didn't come into use until 1911 (a song called "Mr. Jefferson Lord, Play That Barbershop Chord" linked the word barbershop with the quartet sound). That form called for a leading second tenor to sing the melody line, a high tenor to sing the line above the melody, a baritone to sing the line below, and a bass to sing the lowest line. As the minstrel show developed into vaudeville, the quartet was diversified to accommodate comedy acts known as "four acts." The invention of audio recording devices at the end of the nineteenth century also spurred the development of vocal harmonization in quartets and quintets. Then the advent of radio changed the nature of harmony.

The rise of radio at first led to a dwindling of barbershop quartets, just as it initially had an adverse effect on the sale of records. Quartets were increasingly replaced by big bands, jazz ensembles, and torch-song singers in the 1920s and 1930s.

Among the first to experiment with vocal harmonies were the Boswell Sisters, who recorded prolifically in the 1930s, often backed by such swing greats as Benny Goodman and the Dorsey Brothers. The Boswells pioneered the infusion of popular vocalizing with a strong element of jazz, including the instrumental use of voices, jazz phrasing, and the use of a rhythmically spontaneous off-the-beat, or syncopated, swing style that was later imitated by dozens of trios, including the Andrews Sisters. Between 1931 and 1938, the sisters (Helvetia, Connie, and Martha) had at least twenty hit recordings, including "Everybody Loves My Baby," "There'll Be Some Changes Made," and "It Don't Mean a Thing."

The Boswells influenced a number of vocalists and vocal groups, including Ella Fitzgerald, Peggy Lee, Mildred Bailey, and the Mills Brothers, a 1930s quartet who favored the vocal imitation of wind instruments and a heavily rhythm and blues–influenced style. The Mills Brothers were the first black vocal group to gain a large white audience. They also were the most successful American male group of all time, with 71 hit singles on the charts spanning four decades (the Andrews Sisters, with 113 hit singles, were the most successful female group). The Mills Brothers' biggest hit was "Paper Doll," released in May 1942. Other hits during the war years include "You Always Hurt the One You Love," "Till Then," "Lazy River," "My Honey's Lovin' Arms" (recorded with Bing Crosby), and "The Very Thought of You."

Other vocal groups of note include the Ink Spots, who introduced the "talking bass" line and are credited with the "ooh" and "ah" backup style that became *de rigueur* in the 1940s and 1950s, the Modernaires, and the Pied Pipers. The Modernaires had their biggest success as part of the Glenn Miller Orchestra in the early 1940s, after Paula Kelly (a vocalist with Artie Shaw and his band until Shaw abruptly disbanded his orchestra in 1939) joined the group, which then consisted of Kelly, Jerry Gray, and Ray McKinley. Their first hit was a song called "Perfidia." Other Modernaire hits of the 1940s include "Chattanooga Choo Choo," which was the first record ever officially certified as a million seller.

Top: Bing Crosby and the
Boswell Sisters. Middle: The
Four Ink Spots (left to right:
Deek Watson, Hoppy Jones,
Charles Fuqua, and Bill
Kerry), from an appearance
in the 1942 Universal
Pictures film Pardon My
Sarong. Bottom: In the
1940s, the Modernaires
perform "Juke Box
Saturday Night" in
Columbia Pictures'
When You're Smiling.

Tommy Dorsey (with trombone) performs at New York's Hotel Astor in 1940 with Frank Sinatra and the Pied Pipers, featuring female vocalist Jo Stafford.

The Pied Pipers were an eight-member group known for their distinctive phrasing and modern harmonizing. When the group was formed in Hollywood in 1938, it consisted of three smaller vocal groups: The Three Rhythm Kings, The Stafford Sisters, and The Four Esquires. The Pied Pipers had a peripatetic career, moving from Los Angeles to New York to Chicago in search of work in the late 1930s and early 1940s. Along the way they recorded a number of classic pop hits, including several with the young Frank Sinatra. They were first teamed with Sinatra while working with Tommy Dorsey and his orchestra in the early 1940s. Among the hit records they recorded with Sinatra during the war years were "I'll Never Smile Again," "Stardust," "I Guess I'll Have to Dream the Rest," "There Are Such Things," and "Personality." They also had a number of hits without Sinatra, including "Let's Get Away from It All" (with Tommy Dorsey) and "I've Got a Gal in Kalamazoo" (with the Glenn Miller Band).

The End of the Journey

After the war ended and the boys who survived came home, people began the slow process of restoration. By 1946, with victory celebrations firmly behind them, facing the realities of getting back to work and the problems of everyday life, Americans found themselves at the end of the sentimental journey that had kept their spirits up during the war years. Most of the big bands called it quits in 1946, and although a number of them reorganized, it was never the same again. Music had changed radically, and the era of the vocalist had only just begun.

The Mills Brothers, 1943.

The Andrews Sisters

The Andrews Sisters joined the war effort in earnest when war was declared in 1941.

The Andrews Sisters were the most successful female vocal group of the pre-rock era. LaVerne (1915–1967), Maxene (1917–), and Patty (1920–) began performing on the vaudeville circuit in 1931 when Patty was only eleven years old. Inspired by the harmonies and other experimental sounds of the Boswell Sisters, the girls at first imitated the Boswells but eventually developed a sound that was uniquely their own: a clean, fresh, hometown sound touched with a swing rhythm.

During the 1930s, the sisters performed with a number of bands and touring groups, culminating with Leon Blasco's band in 1936–1937 (where they were paid the whopping sum of thirty-five dollars a week).

They made their radio debut that same year on Billy Swanson's program broadcast live from the Edison Hotel. Though they sang only one song, "Sleepytime Down South," the broadcast piqued the interest of Decca Records president Dave Kapp, who signed them to their first recording contract within the week. Though their first recording went unnoticed, their second, "Bei Mir Bist Du Schon," became a number one song in January 1938. By the end of that year, the Andrew Sisters were earning one thousand dollars doing seven shows a week at the New York Paramount. By 1939, they had six titles on the charts. They were young and fresh and had a harmonic style that filled the nation's need for simplicity and ease.

From 1938 through the war years, they recorded dozens of hits, including "Hold Tight—Hold Tight," "Boogie Woogie Bugle Boy," "Don't Sit Under the Apple Tree," "Straighten Up and Fly Right," and "Rum and Coca Cola." They recorded twenty-three singles with Bing Crosby during their career and collaborated with many other musical artists, including Guy Lombardo, Jimmy Dorsey, Danny Kaye, Dick Haymes, Carmen Miranda, and Burl Ives.

When war was declared in 1941, the Andrews Sisters joined the war effort, visiting more army, navy, and air force bases than any other vocal group, singing on Armed Forces Radio programs, and making special recordings for troops stationed overseas. Their 1940s film contract with Universal Studios led to appearances in a number of wartime musicals, including *Follow the Boys, Private Buckaroo, Buck Privates in the Navy,* and *Swing Time.* They sang their 1944 hit "Don't Fence Me In" with Bing Crosby when they appeared in the film *Hollywood Canteen.* During the war years, the Andrews Sisters had thirty-eight hit songs, including nine recorded with Crosby, and by war's end they had sold more than thirty million records.

After the war the sisters were back at the Paramount, earning twenty thousand dollars a week this time around. Postwar hits included "Is You Is or Is You Ain't My Baby," "Beat Me Daddy, Eight to the Bar," and "Get Your Kicks on Route 66." From 1937 until the trio disbanded in 1954, the Andrews Sisters recorded hundreds of records, including nineteen gold records. In the 1960s, the sisters began making appearances on television, but that came to an end in 1967 when LaVerne died. During their career, the Andrews Sisters sold seventy-five million records, recorded more than eighteen thousand songs, and appeared in twenty-two films.

Left to right: LaVerne, Patti, and Maxene, who began performing together in 1931.

Suggested Listening

Benny Goodman

King Porter Stomp (written by Jelly Roll Morton, 1924; arranged by Fletcher Henderson, 1935)

Blue Skies (written by Irving Berlin, 1927; arranged by Fletcher Henderson, 1935)

Between the Devil and the Deep Blue Sea (written by Harold Arlen, 1931)

Life Goes to a Party (arranged by Harry James, 1937)

Stompin' at the Savoy (written by Benny Goodman, 1936)

Glenn Miller

I Got Rhythm (written by George Gershwin, 1937)

Moonlight Serenade (written by Glenn Miller, 1939)

In the Mood (written by Joe Garland, 1930; recorded 1939)

Sunrise Serenade (written by Frankie Carle, 1939)

Little Brown Jug (written by Joseph E. Winner, 1869; arranged by Bill Finegan, 1939)

Tuxedo Junction (written by Erskine Hawkins, recorded 1934)

Pennsylvania 6-5000 (arranged by Jerry Gray, 1940)

Chattanooga Choo Choo (with the Modernaires)

Tommy Dorsey

I'm Getting Sentimental over You (written by George Bassman and Ned Washington, 1932)

Marie

Let's Get Away from It All (with the Pied Pipers)

Jimmy Dorsey

Tangerine (written by Johnny Mercer and Victor Schertzinger, 1942)

In a Sentimental Mood (written by Duke Ellington, 1935; arranged by Bobby Byrne, 1936)

Green Eyes

Harry James

You Made Me Love You

How High the Moon

I've Heard That Song Before

I Don't Want to Walk Without You

Les Brown

Just One of Those Things

I've Got My Love to Keep Me Warm

My Dreams Are Getting Better All the Time

Bing Crosby

Moonlight Becomes You

A Pocketful of Dreams

Swingin' on a Star

25

Frank Sinatra
All or Nothing at All
I'll Never Smile Again
Let's Get Away from It All
Stardust (with Tommy Dorsey
and the Pied Pipers)

Doris Day
Day After Day
It Could Happen to You
My Dreams Are Getting Better
All the Time
We'll Be Together Again

Dinah Shore
Yes, My Darling Daughter
How Sweet You Are
Blues in the Night
I'll Walk Alone

Kate Smith
God Bless America (written by
Irving Berlin, 1939)
Did You Ever See a Dream
Walking?
I'll Be Seeing You

Perry Como
If I Loved You
Till the End of Time

Peggy Lee
Why Don't You Do Right?

The Andrews Sisters
Bei Mir Bist Du Schon
Boogie Woogie Bugle Boy
Straighten Up and Fly Right

Photo Credits

AP/Wide World Photos:
pp. 11 bottom, 41 top

Archive Photos:
pp. 2, 7 top, 9, 12 top, 28, 34–35,
51, 55 top, 57 bottom, 59

The Bettmann Archive:
pp. 11 top, 12 bottom, 19 bottom, 20, 30, 41 bottom, 57 top,
63 bottom, 65

Frank Driggs Collection:
pp. 15, 17 top, 32–33, 39, 46, 53,
56, 64, 66

FPG International:
pp. 19 top, 29, 37 top, 38, 58

**Lester Glassner Collection/
Neal Peters:**
p. 60

© Globe Photos:
pp. 35 top, 54

© NBC/Globe Photos:
pp. 26, 43 bottom

Neal Peters Collection:
p. 50

Photofest:
pp. 16–17, 21, 24, 27, 37 bottom,
42, 43 top, 44, 45, 47 top &
bottom, 48, 52, 63 top, 67

© SMP/Globe Photos:
p. 7 bottom

Further Reading

Hemming, Roy and David Hajdu. *Classic Pop*. New York: Newmarket Press, 1991.

Schuller, Gunther. *The Swing Era: The Development of Jazz 1930–1945*. New York: Oxford University Press, 1989.

Simon, George T. *The Big Bands*. London: Schirmer Books/ Macmillan, 4th edition, 1981.

Warner, Jay. *American Singing Groups: A History 1940–1990*. New York: Billboard Books/Watson-Guptill Publications, 1992.

White, Mark. *Big Bands*. London: Frederick Warne Publishers, 1978.

Wilder, Alec. *American Popular Song: The Great Innovators 1900–1950*.

London: Oxford University Press, 1972.

Index

"All or Nothing at All," 48
"Amapola," 36
American Society of Composers, Authors and Publishers, 14, 15, 18
Andrews Sisters, 62, 66–67, 66, 67
Annie Get Your Gun (film), 47
Arlen, Harold, 14
Armed Services Bands, 13, 31
Armstrong, Louis, 23

Bailey, Mildred, 44, 62
Barnet, Charlie, 17
Barton, Eileen, 57
"Beat Me Daddy, Eight to the Bar," 67
"Bei Mir Bist Du Schon," 66
The Bells of St. Mary's (film), 45
Berigan, Bunny, 27
Berlin, Irving, 14
"Blues in the Night," 27, 53
"Blue Skies," 27
"Boogie Woogie Bugle Boy," 67
Boswell Sisters, 61, 62, 63, 66
Brown, Les, 18, 28, 29, 39, 40, 50
"Buttons and Bows," 53

Cabanne, Mimi, 41
Carle, Frankie, 29, 39, 42, 42
Carnegie Hall (New York), 27
"Chattanooga Choo Choo," 31, 62
"Ciribiribin," 18
"Come Fly With Me," 49
Como, Perry, 42, 45, 56–57, 56, 57
Crosby, Bing, 17, 42, 44–45, 44, 45, 49, 55, 56, 62, 63, 67
Crosby, Bob, 13, 17, 29, 50

Day, Doris, 17, 21, 28, 40, 40, 42, 50–51, 50, 51
"Day After Day," 50
Dorsey, Jimmy, 11, 15, 17, 22, 23, 29, 29, 36–37, 37, 61, 67
Dorsey, Tommy, 11, 16, 17, 18, 19, 20, 22, 22, 29, 32, 36–37, 37, 38, 49, 56, 61, 64, 64
Duchin, Eddy, 13, 17

Eberly, Bob, 36

Fitzgerald, Ella, 62
"Fools Rush In," 38
Forrest, Helen, 19, 27, 32–33, 38, 39, 42, 58, 60, 60
"For Sentimental Reasons," 36
Four Jills in a Jeep (Film), 15

Gershwin, George, 14, 26
Gershwin, Ira, 14
Gleason, Jackie, 37
Glen Island Casino (New York), 11, 25, 30, 36
"God Bless America," 54
Going My Way (film), 45
Goldkette, Jean, 36
Goodman, Benny, 11, 16, 17, 22, 25, 26–27, 26, 27, 29, 30, 31, 32, 38, 58, 60, 61
Grable, Betty, 32, 38, 60
"Green Eyes," 36

Hart, Lorenz, 14
Haymes, Dick, 38, 42, 55, 60, 67
Haymes, Joe, 36
Heidt, Horace, 17, 29, 39, 40, 41, 42
Henderson, Fletcher, 27, 31
Herman, Woody, 16, 17, 29, 32
Hoboken Four, 48, 48
"Hold Tight—Hold Tight," 67
Hollywood, 16–17, 45, 50, 64
Hope, Bob, 40, 45
Howard, Eddy, 47
"How High the Moon," 48
"How Long Has This Been Goin' On?," 27
Hutton, Betty, 12, 42, 43, 47

"I Cried for You," 60
"I Don't Want to Walk Without You," 32, 38, 60
"If I Loved You," 56
"I Got a Gal in Kalamazoo," 31
"I Had the Craziest Dream," 38, 60
"I'll Be Seeing You," 45, 54
"I'll Never Smile Again," 49, 64
"I'll Walk Alone," 53
"I'm Getting Sentimental over You," 18
Ink Spots, 63
"In the Mood," 31
"Ishkabibble," 34, 35
"I've Got My Love to Keep Me Warm," 39
"I've Got the World on a String," 49
"I've Heard that Song Before," 38, 60

James, Harry, 11, 16–17, 17, 18, 19, 27, 29, 32–33, 36, 38–39, 38, 39, 48, 60
"Juke Box Saturday Night," 31
"Just One of Those Things," 39

Kallen, Kitty, 15, 36
Kay Kyser's Kollege of Musical Knowledge (radio), 10, 34, 35
Kelly, Paula, 62
Kenton, Stan, 17
Kern, Jerome, 14
"King Porter Stomp," 27
King Sisters, 40

Krupa, Gene, 16, 17, 27
Kyser, Kay, *11*, 17, 29, 30, 34–35, *35*, 41

Las Vegas Nights (film), 16, *20*
Lee, Peggy, *17*, 21, 27, 42, 45, 58, *58, 59*, 60, 62
Let's Dance (radio), 10, 26, 27
Lewis, Ted, 26
"Little Brown Jug," 31
Lombardo, Guy, *12*, 25, 29, *57*, 67

Make-Believe Ballroom (radio), 10, 38
"Marie," 36
McKinley, Ray, 62
Meadowbrook Ballroom (New Jersey), 25, 30, 31
Mercer, Johnny, 14, 34, 49
Miller, Glenn, 11, 12, 13, 17, 18, 19, 22, *24*, 25, 29, 30–31, *30*, 62, 64
Mills Brothers, 62, *65*
Miranda, Carmen, 67
Modernaires, 31, 62, *63*
"Moonlight Becomes You," 45
"Moonlight Serenade," 18, 31
Music Makers, *19*, *32–33*

"The Nearness of You," 38
Nichols, Red, 36
Noble, Ray, 31
Noone, Jimmy, 26
Norvo, Red, 27

O'Connell, Helen, 36, 42
"Once in a While," 36
Orchestra Wives (film), 12, 16
"Over There," 8

Page, Patti, 27
Palomar Ballroom (Hollywood), 11, 26, 27, 30
"Paper Doll," 62
Paradise Restaurant (New York), 25, 31
Paramount Theater (New York), 44, 66
"Pennsylvania 6-5000," 31
"Perfidia," 62
Pied Pipers, 36, 56, 62, 64, *64*
"A Pocketful of Dreams," 45
Pollack, Ben, 26, 31, 36
Porter, Cole, 14

Radio, 10, 13, 14–21, 25, 31, 32, 38, 40, 45, 54, 67
Rainbow Room (New York), 31
Raye, Martha, 9
Rey, Alvino, 13, 40

Rodgers, Richard, 14
Roseland State Ballroom (Boston), 25, 31
Royalties, 14, 15
"Rum and Coca Cola," 67

"Sentimental Journey," 18, 28, 39, 50
Shaw, Artie, 13, 16, 17, 29, 38, 60, 62
"Shoofly Pie and Apple Pandowdy," 53
Shore, Dinah, 42, *52, 53, 53*
Sinatra, Frank, 17, 19, *20*, 21, *21*, 36, 38, 42, 45, *46*, 48–49, *48*, *49*, 53, 56, 64, *64*
"Skylark," 60
Smith, Kate, 42, 53, 54, *54*
"So Rare," 37
Springtime in the Rockies (film), 32
Stafford, Jo, 36, 42, 56, 60, *64*
Stage Door Canteen (film), 16, 17
"Stardust," 49, 64
"Sunrise Serenade," 39, 42
"Swingin' on a Star," 45

"Tangerine," 36
Television, 37, 40, 53, 67
"There Are Such Things," 36
"This Love of Mine," 36, 49
Thornhill, Claude, 13
"Till the End of Time," 56
"Till Then," 62
Tilton, Martha, 27, *43*
Touring, 13, 32, 46
"Tuxedo Junction," 31

USO shows, 13, 34

Vallee, Rudy, 49

Walker, Nancy, 16–17
Webb, Jack, *58*
Weems, Ted, 13, 56
"The White Cliffs of Dover," 54
Whiteman, Paul, 25, 26, 36, 44, *55*
Winter Wonderland (film), 16
Wood, Donna, 41
World War II, 8, 10, *11*, 13, 14, 16, 18

"You Always Hurt the One You Love," 62
"You Made Me Love You," 38
Your Hit Parade (radio), 10, 37, 53
"Yours," 36